# FLYING COLOURS

Best Sellers in Adult Colouring Books with Stress Relieving Patterns, Mandalas, Animals, Flowers and other Beautiful Designs

FLYING COLOURS

# Free Stuff?
# Yes Please!

Like free stuff? So do we! Come check out
the site and get yourself some freebies!

*www.motherdearestbooks.com/bonus*

It is with great pleasure that we thank you for purchasing our adult colouring book. We find that there is nothing more relaxing than sitting down with a box of coloured pencils and colouring beautiful images for hours. Whether you enjoy intricate patterns or ornately drawn animals we are certain you will be extremely pleased with the images inside this book. Please relax, clear your mind and colour to your hearts content.

Enjoy!

Mother Dearest Colouring Books

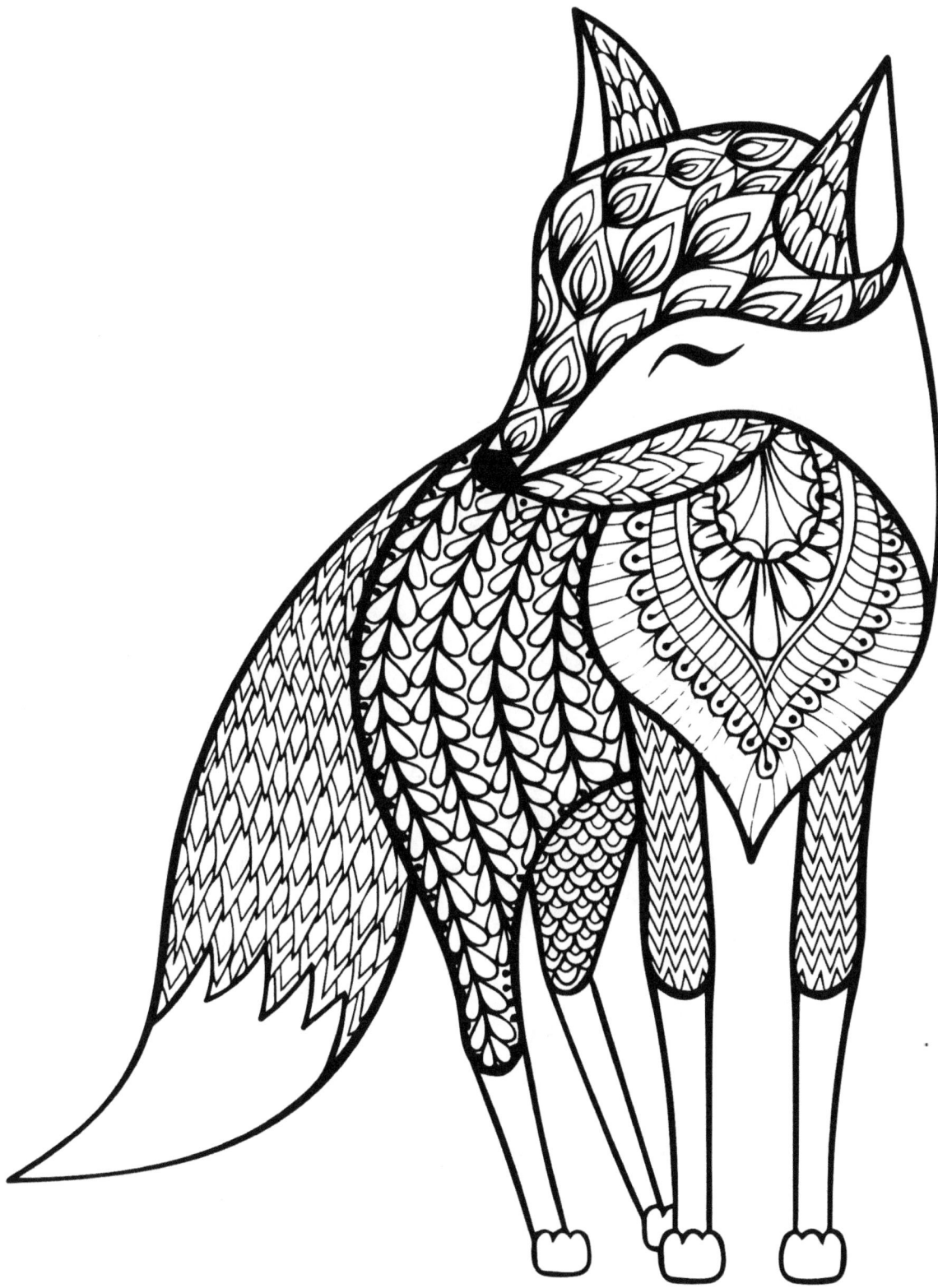

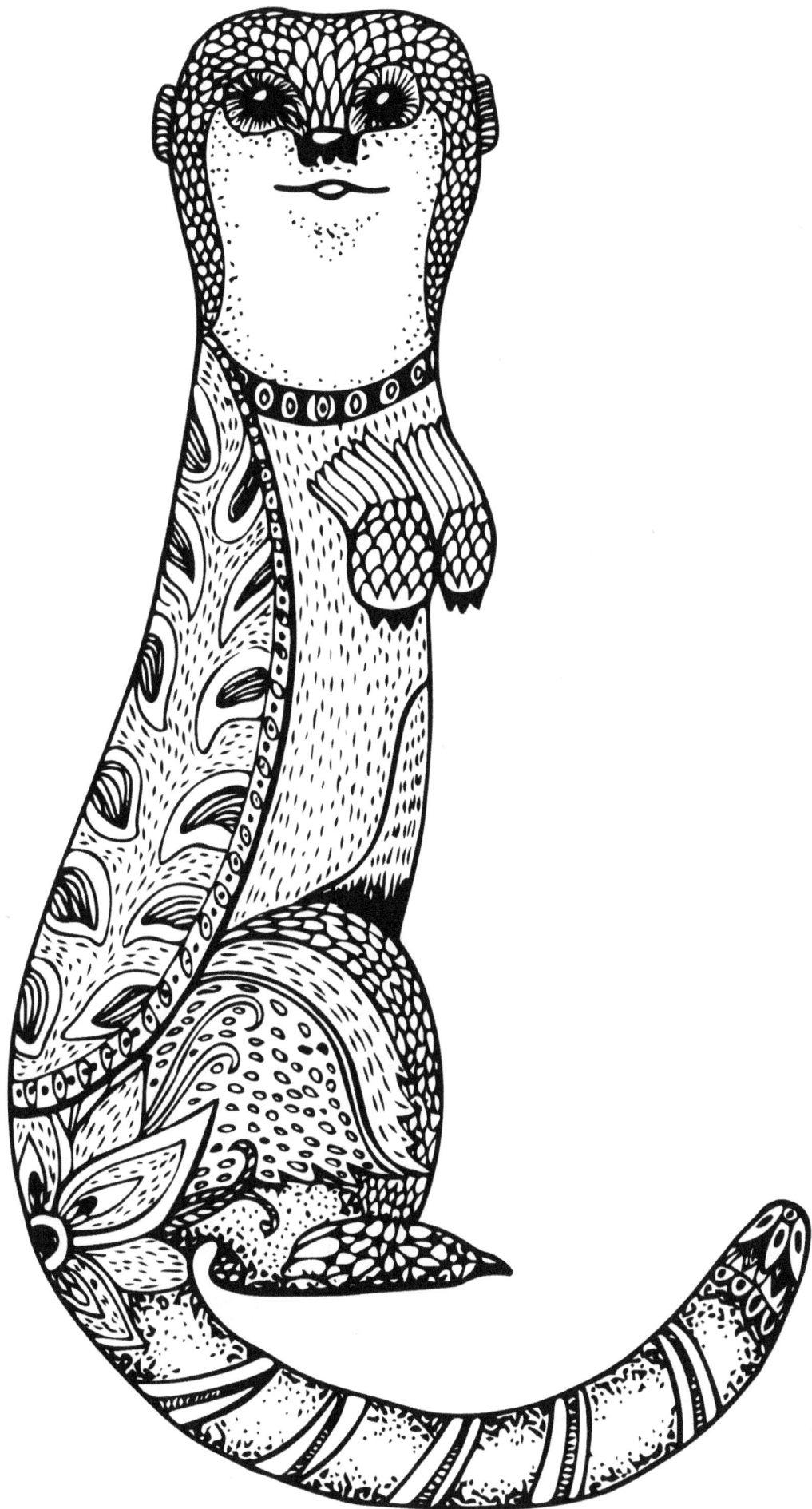

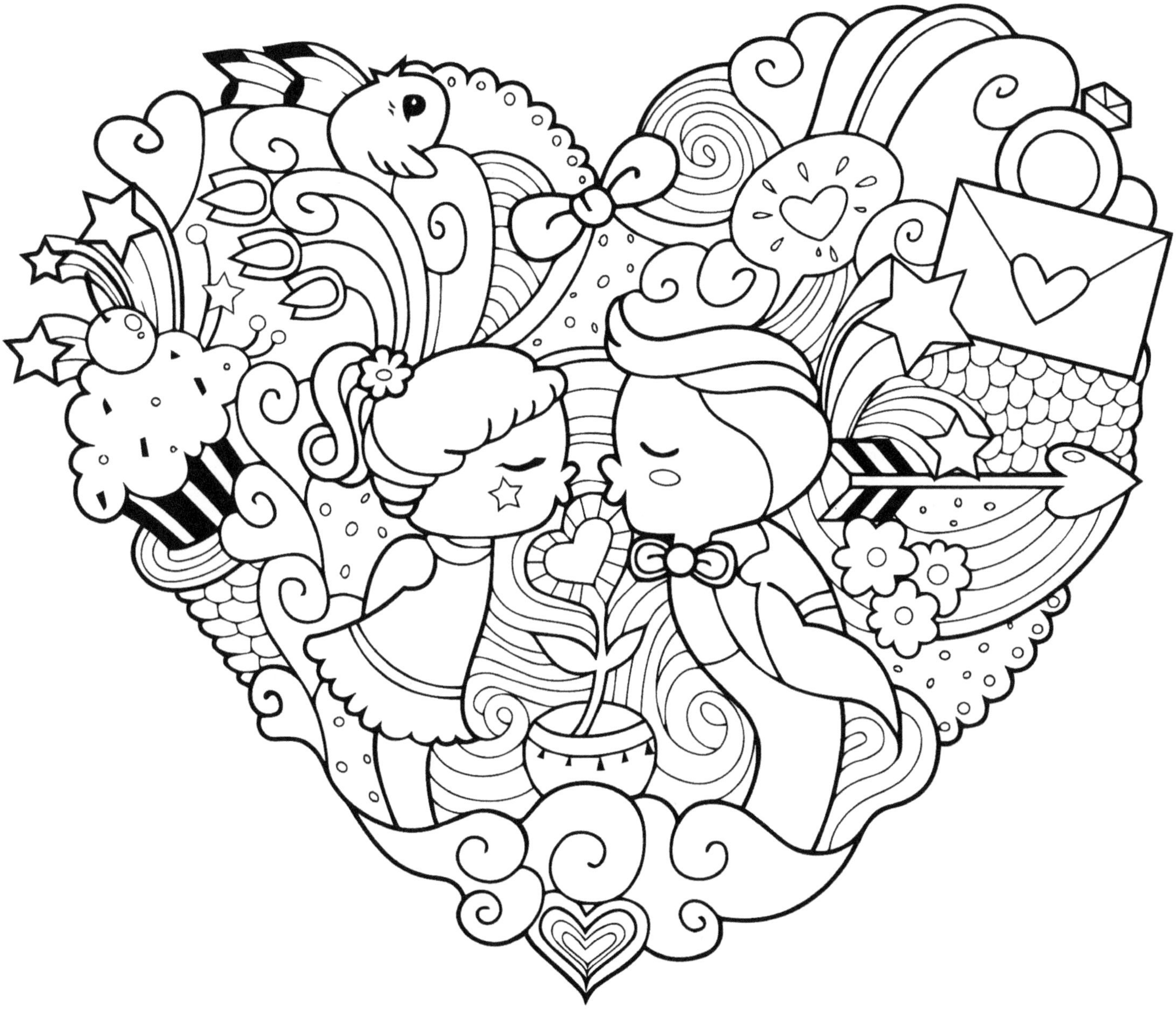

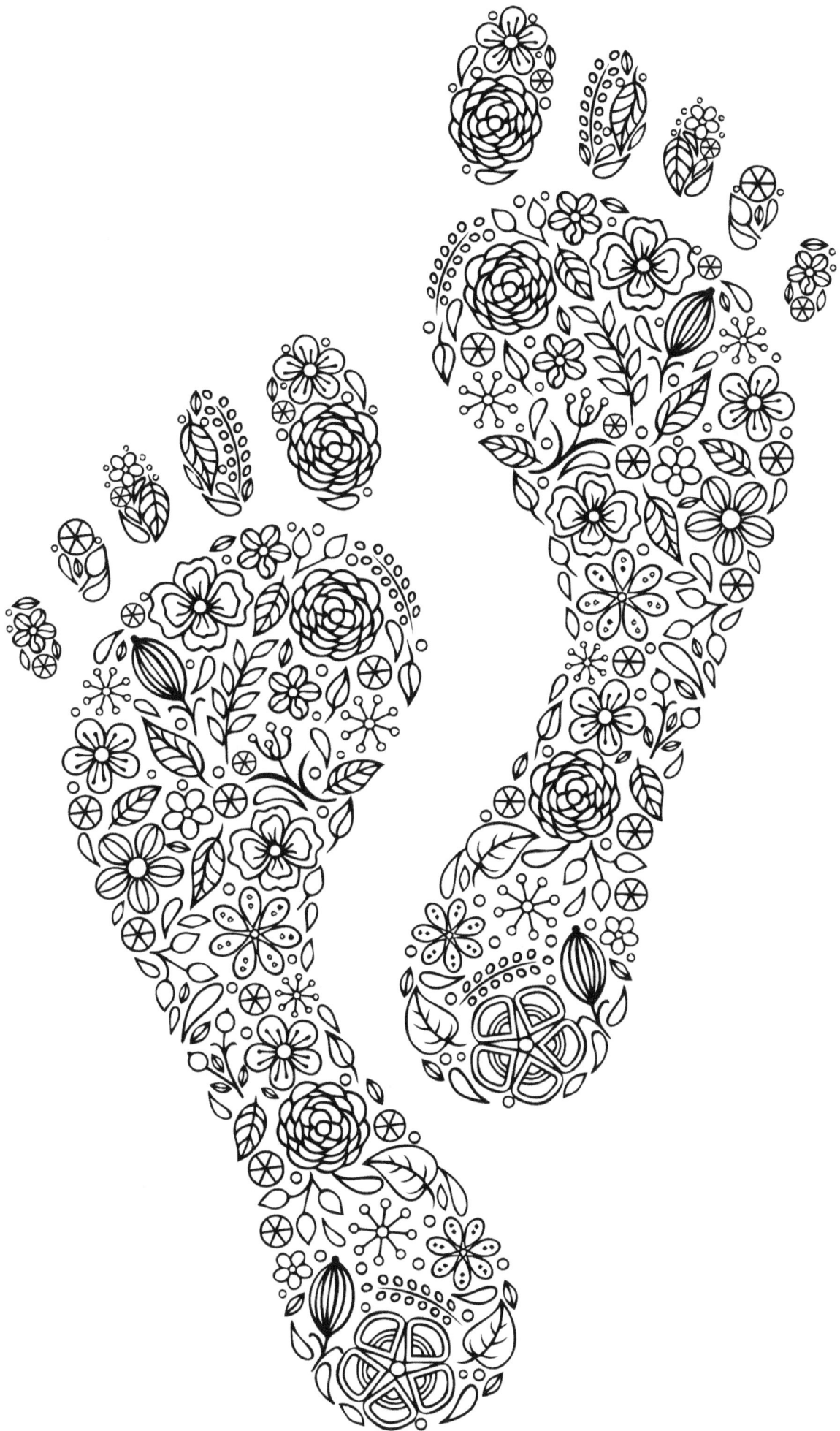

www.ingramcontent.com/pod-product-compliance
Lightning Source LLC
Chambersburg PA
CBHW081538040426
42447CB00014B/3425